30 SECONDS THAT CAN CHANGE YOUR LIFE

30 SECONDS THAT CAN CHANGE YOUR LIFE

Learning to Use the Unused Moments of Life

Dr. Gerald D. Robison

ISBN (paperback): 978-0-9822607-3-9
ISBN (ebook): 978-0-9822607-4-6

Book design and production by www.AuthorSuccess.com
Cover art by iStock

Printed in the United States of America

To my big brother, Corwin M. Robison II. I've known him all my life and have always looked to him for various forms of advice and counsel. His insights and wisdom have helped me and are always appreciated. At one time we grew up together, then apart . . . and now we grow old together. Thanks for your input and assistance!

Contents

INTRODUCTION: Thirty Seconds That Can Change Your Life   1

CHAPTER 1:   I Don't Have the Time for That   5

CHAPTER 2:   A Stitch in Time Saves Nine   11

CHAPTER 3:   Use Common Sense   17

CHAPTER 4:   Where Did the Time Go?   23

CHAPTER 5:   The Lifetime Countdown Watch   29

CHAPTER 6:   What You Can and Can't Do with Time   35

CHAPTER 7:   You Can't MAKE Time, But You Can FIND It   43

CHAPTER 8:   The "Thirty-Second Rule"   49

CHAPTER 9:   Time Might Be Infinite … But Not YOURS   57

CHAPTER 10: Know Yourself and Wrestle with Yourself   65

CHAPTER 11: The Eisenhower What!?!   73

CONCLUSION: Ten Important Things That Can Be Done   81
             in Thirty Seconds

As a bonus, I wanted to share helpful lists of what you can accomplish in 30-seconds elsewhere.

Suggestion   86

Appendix   87

Bedroom   89

Tape Gun   92

Plastic Bag   94

Vacuum   96

Garden Hose   98

Shovel   100

Trash Can   102

Mobile Phone   104

Label Maker   106

Flashlight   108

Waiting in Line   110

About the Author   113

Thirty Seconds That Can Change Your Life

No matter your age, everyone needs a little help from time to time—whether it's with homework, business, housekeeping, or car-care. Sometimes we just have to ask for help . . . and sometimes we're successful while at other times we're not. Why is that?

If you ask someone for some time, they may be hesitant to give up an hour, a half hour, or maybe even ten minutes. Everyone is so busy, and asking for their time is an inconvenience or an interference to them. In fact, they might even stop to think and ponder if you ask for as little as five minutes. Why? People are consumed with their own agendas, and everyone has their own "to do" list without giving away their time to you.

Even if you say, "It will only take a few minutes," that's undefined enough that they may decline. Unfortunately, the experience of too many people is that an undefined amount of time turns into a project, and they assume that they're going to end up shouting, "If I'd known it was going to take this long, I would've said no!"

But, asking someone for thirty seconds is like asking for a penny. It's nothing to them; it's too small to pay attention to. As a result, almost everyone is open to giving you thirty seconds.

In the grand tapestry of life, there are countless threads woven with moments that are both monumental and minute. Yet, amidst the hustle and bustle of our daily existence, it's the seemingly insignificant thirty-second intervals that often hold the power to transform our world. These fleeting half-minutes, like precious grains of sand slipping through an hourglass, can shape our destiny, catalyze profound change, or merely offer a momentary respite from the chaos of life.

In the following pages, we will embark on a journey to explore the incredible potential locked within those brief overlooked moments, imploring you to seize the seconds and change your life one half-minute at a time. For in these miniscule but mighty increments of moments lies the key to unlocking a life of fulfillment, lasting impact, and even peace of mind.

The book *Cheaper by The Dozen* was required reading in my early school years, and I was quite taken by the father in that story, who was an acute observer of time and motion. I wanted to be an 'efficiency expert' like him. Although I studied and received degrees in psychology, sociology, counseling, theology, and education, I always missed not studying 'efficiency methods,' even though I kept pursuing how I and others could do more in a way that was better and faster. So, this book is my effort to finally answer the question: "How can I help everyday people accomplish more in everyday life and feel good about it?"

This book is written to help you, the reader, to develop a more pragmatic, systematic, and organized lifestyle. And it's done without using any more of your precious time.

You see, I realized we all have little crumbs of time all around us that go unused. What we forget is that if you get enough crumbs, you'll soon have a cookie. If you collect enough raindrops, you can take a shower. If you collect enough bricks, you can build a mansion.

What I mean is, if you adjust your time that is already fleeting into the past, and use those snippets of time effectively, your life can become more. What do I mean your life can become "more?"

- ○ You'll find time to do more
- ○ You'll find time to go more
- ○ You'll find time to say more in the meaningful areas of life

Just fill those small otherwise empty and unused packets of time that we tend to let drift by ignored.

This applies no matter your age or your generational level. If you are a young student there are a lot of things you *want* to do, but the things you *have* to do become like a weight that keeps you down.

Young adults, as high school or university students, have so many things clamoring for their time and attention. How can you get the time you need to do the things you must?

This book will help.

Young couples with babies are always searching for, and in need of, 'more time' but don't know where to find it. You can't make time, so how do you accomplish all that's needed?

This book will help.

For those who have given themselves to homemaking, career, service, or other endeavors . . . we're all looking for more time. But it doesn't help because there's still only sixty seconds to every minute and sixty minutes to every hour, and they all seem 'taken.'

This book will help.

It's not just us old geezers who wonder how many more days, hours, minutes, or seconds we have left. Everyone can use their time better. If we will just reshape our thinking, it can reshape our lives. **This book will help.**

If you collect enough thirty-second moments that are passing into your personal history empty and unused, you'll find larger segments of time freed up for what makes your life 'more.'

I've written each chapter to be short, succinct, and meaningful. They are written to help you think about your life and how you spend each moment you have.

At the end of each chapter, I list thirty things you can do in thirty seconds. I've listed them in many areas of your life, including home, work, and more. They are not meant to be a checklist, whereby if you do all of them, you'll be happier. No, they are merely there for you to see that there is a lot you can get done in the time you have but don't use.

Make your own lists. Contemplate, ponder, and discover that everyone's day has only twenty-four hours . . . and how many of those you have is limited. But it may surprise you what you can get done in mere moments. Before now, you have probably convinced yourself that tasks took too long, but I challenge you to try some of the many things you can do in just thirty seconds that you would have left otherwise empty.

I hope that you'll discover the joy of doing a great many things in just thirty seconds. Reclaim your moments so your days and years will be more enjoyable . . . and do so without using more time.

I Don't Have the Time for That

If you walk past a construction site and pick up a lone, feeble brick, no one notices; no one cares. A brick is hardly anything that matters. No single brick can do much, but with enough of them, a mansion, a city, and a civilization can be built. What I want to show you is that you can build a better life by picking up and using simple thirty-second segments of time . . . and just keep doing that over and over again.

In a world that often seems to race ahead at an unforgiving pace, where our days are a whirlwind of obligations, dreams deferred, and the ever-elusive pursuit of a better tomorrow, it's easy to overlook the transformative power that lies within the tiniest fragments of time.

Yet, it is in these fleeting thirty-second intervals, nestled inconspicuously within the tapestry of our existence, which rests the potential to shape our lives in ways profound and enduring.

Welcome to a journey of discovery; an adventure where we'll unlock the secrets of change, growth, and personal evolution, all in the span of just half a minute. In the following pages, we will embark on a remarkable quest to harness these often-neglected moments, weaving them into the fabric of our daily lives to create lasting, positive transformation.

This book is about seizing the seconds, rewiring our habits, and embracing the immense potential that resides within the next thirty seconds of your life. Prepare to embark on a journey of incremental but monumental change as we explore the art of transforming your life thirty seconds at a time.

Our world is so fast paced that I often find myself wanting a time out. But that's when I put off, delay, or ignore the 'small things' so I can save time for the big ones. Only later do I find that all my small things ganged up and formed a club demanding as much time as other large tasks. When I wasn't looking, they formed into an overbearing task awaiting me to come and deal with them.

You see, untangling a single strand of spaghetti would take no time at all and can be easily put off. But when put off with many other spaghetti strands, they soon become entangled, sizeable, unmanageable, and then you need a spoon to wind them up or a knife to cut them into bite-sized pieces, either of which is time-consuming.

Oh, the irony of it: the small things I put off in order to save time for the big things have now become another big thing that demands more time! How do I save myself from this obnoxious cycle and get more done in my life?

Why Is This So Important?

Finding a way to use thirty-second segments that are empty, useless, and barren frees up other time for the more important things. When you get to be my age, you may beg God for more time. But what if he asks, "What did you do with the time I gave you?"

Nearing the end of my lifespan, I've come to appreciate 'time' more than ever. There is more I want to do … more that I want to say … more that I want to write. I could ask God for more, but He might question me on how I used what I had, and I'm sorry to say it was not used for maximum efficiency and effectiveness. If I had done so, would my jobs have been done at a higher level? Would my work have been better executed and with greater results? I like to think it would, but what about you?

If you have a job, maybe that's a great place to start. Do you have an office? Okay, how can you change your habits there so that you use a simple span of thirty seconds for something useful? If you can do so, then you'll begin to manage freeing up small pockets of time for something useful and allow more time for the bigger things. REALLY?

Yes!

So, let's pause for a practical lesson. What can someone do in their office in thirty seconds?

Thirty Things in Thirty Seconds
You can do in the OFFICE

These thirty-second items can make your workplace more efficient and even more enjoyable. Don't be limited to the ones I have listed, and don't worry if some take a little longer. Either stay an extra moment to get it done, or just do more in your next thirty-second break.

1. **Your Desk:** Organize stray papers, pens, or other items that can be tidied up.

2. **Your Calendar:** Consult and review upcoming meetings or deadlines and review upcoming to-do items.

3. **Your Email:** Take a moment and quickly delete the junk and save only the important new emails.

4. **Your Email:** There are a lot of emails that just don't take time. Write or reply to a short message.

5. **A Moment for Yourself:** Take a moment to relieve stress: take a deep breath and stretch.

6. **Your Task List:** Update, plan, add, and delete items on your to-do list. Keep track of your progress.

7. **A News Headline:** Check for a quick news update or industry headline. Don't read the whole item; usually two or three paragraphs are really enough to get the big idea.

8. **Your Water Bottle:** Fill up your water bottle or grab a fresh drink.

9. **Your Notifications:** Look at your phone or computer notifications for any important updates. Don't linger on them; update yourself and move on.

10. **Your Colleagues:** Share a brief greeting or catch up with a coworker for a moment. Remember, it's a greeting, not a discussion, and not a planning time. Just acknowledge them and with a few spoken words and move on.

11. **Your Cables:** Neatly arrange or secure any tangled computer cables or chargers.

12. **Your To-Do List:** Adjust it! Add, delete, or substitute items according to their priority and timeliness.

13. **Your Keyboard:** Clean it! Use a small brush or compressed air to remove crumbs or dust from your keyboard.

14. **Your Ink or Paper:** Check your printer. Refill or replace the ink, paper, or toner as needed.

15. **Your Trash:** Come on, it just doesn't take that long.

16. **Your Files:** File any documents or papers that are scattered on your desk.

17. **Your Surfaces:** Use a disinfecting wipe to clean your desk. Tidy up office drawers and arrange items neatly.

18. **Your Lighting:** Get better visibility. Turn on or adjust desk lamps and set a timer for an upcoming task, meeting, or reminder.

19. **Your Computer Desktop:** Remove any unnecessary icons or shortcuts from your computer desktop.

20. **Your Wiring:** Bundle or hide loose wires. A modern office is not complete without wires, but they don't have to be obvious or cluttering.

21. **Your Books:** Quickly organize any books or manuals on your desk or shelves.

22. **Your Sticky Notes:** Cull or make sticky notes with tasks and reminders.

23. **Your Supplies:** Be sure you have enough office supplies like pens, paper, and staples.

24. **Your Documents:** Get documents ready for your next meeting or task.

25. **Your Business Cards:** Cull, add, update, or file any business cards you have collected.

26. **Your Environment:** Set your office thermostat and air flow or adjust a fan to a comfortable setting.

27. **Project Status:** Glance over your project status and update any notes on progress or delays.

28. **Your Phone:** Wipe down your office phone/headset to—remove fingerprints and dust.

29. **Your furniture:** Move chairs (blinds, curtains, or other furniture) so that guests don't have sunlight in their eyes. Make it comfortable for all—both you and them when they are in your office.

30. **Your windows & mirrors:** Keep a little glass cleaner handy. Streaks, smears, glare, dirt, cobwebs don't make a good impression.

CHAPTER 2

A Stitch in Time Saves Nine

This is a quote from *Poor Richard's Almanac*, written by Benjamin Franklin. Wise sayings are often called 'proverbs.' A proverb is a short pithy saying that states a wise bit of advice. This one shares the wisdom of doing something now before the problem grows and more time and effort are needed to accomplish it at a later time.

You may or may not be religious, but I want you to know there is a whole section of the Bible that is filled with wisdom for daily life. It's even called Proverbs. Proverbs have always struck me as wise and witty sayings that can help smooth the wrinkles of life. There is another spot in the Bible where I found helpful insight. There, it says that I'm to be . . .

". . . redeeming the time, because the days are evil."
Ephesians 5:16 [NKJV]

While I'm certain it was not looking at all the pieces of email that I have been too busy to deal with, I do have the habit of just collecting them in my inbox. The problem is that they have now grown, seemingly multiplied, and pour out overflowing the boundaries of that same inbox. So, the adage still applies: *redeem the time*!

'Redeem the time' is a phrase often associated with making the most of your time and opportunities. It's a concept that encourages people to use their time wisely and productively, especially in pursuit of their goals, personal growth, and meaningful activities. The idea behind redeeming the time is to avoid wasting it on unimportant or frivolous pursuits, and instead focus on activities that have value, purpose, and significance. To 'redeem' is to 'buy back.' The phrase is often attributed to the Bible, specifically Ephesians 5:16 in the New Testament, highlighted above. In a religious context, it carries the additional meaning of living a righteous and morally upright life in a world that is perceived as sinful or corrupted.

In a more general sense, 'redeeming the time' means taking advantage of the opportunities and moments that life presents, being mindful of how you allocate your time, and using it in a way that aligns with your priorities and values. It emphasizes the importance of not procrastinating, setting meaningful goals, and taking action to achieve them.

Have you realized that you and Elon Musk have the same amount of time each and every day? How does he accomplish so much in the same amount of time you have? Yes, he has a lot of help, but he also has learned a lot about redeeming his time.

So now I ask the pertinent question: "How do I redeem my time?"

And you should be asking the same query for yourself: how can *you* redeem your time?

For me, the answer was: thirty seconds at a time.

And I'm betting this can be a helpful remedy for you, too!

Time is like gravel . . . it's all around us, but it's small and it's manageable. You can find it almost anywhere and everywhere, and nobody seems to notice or care if you take some small pieces for yourself along the way.

There are thirty-second slots of time at home, in the car, and while shopping, eating, and playing. There are thirty-second pieces of time at work, church, in the yard, the garage, your bedroom, and in the bath. They are everywhere, which means you can pick them up anywhere and use them for yourself, and no one seems to care or begrudge you for doing it. Those are the pieces of time you will learn to redeem.

How? Let's suppose for a moment you need a snack. (No, don't get up to grab one right now!) You may walk to your pantry to find something appealing. While you're standing there, is there something you can get done within half a minute?

On the next page, I've listed thirty things I can do in my pantry within thirty seconds. Let's take a look:

Thirty Things in Thirty Seconds
You can do in the PANTRY

These thirty-second items can make your pantry more efficient and even more enjoyable. Don't be limited to the ones I've listed, and don't worry if some take a little longer. Either stay an extra moment to get it done, or just do more in your next thirty-second break.

These quick actions can help to keep your pantry organized, clean, and well-stocked!

1. **Your soups:** Make them visible so you know what's there.

2. **Your cereals:** Arrange them so that it is easy to see what's available.

3. **Your fruits/veggies:** Arrange cans so they are easy to find and don't spoil.

4. **Your paper goods:** If you have paper bags, stack them in an orderly fashion.

5. **Your cans of soda:** Organize your soda according to kind, flavor, size.

6. **Your bottles:** Give a sense of order to them.

7. **Your plastic bags:** Create a place for all of those plastic bags. Store them all in one.

8. **Your unusual and small items:** Don't lose them or make them eyesores. Think about using fabric boxes for organizing.

9. **Your Snacks:** Put them in one place so you'll know where to look when you want one.

10. **Your Meals:** Take a moment to think about what ingredients you have and what you might want to make for an upcoming meal.

11. **Your Inventory:** Quickly assess what staples you're running low on, like flour, sugar, or canned goods. Jot down a quick note on what you need to replenish soon.

12. **Your Surfaces:** Use a paper towel or cloth to quickly clean any spills or crumbs on pantry shelves.

13. **Your Expired Items:** Identify and pull out any items that may be past their prime and need to be discarded.

14. **Your Visibility:** Move things around to make sure the items you use most often are easily accessible.

15. **Your Spices:** Arrange spice jars or containers by type or size for easier access.

16. **Your Baking Supplies: Group** baking supplies like flour, sugar, and baking soda together on one shelf.

17. **Your Pests:** Look for any signs of pests or insects and address issues if needed.

18. **Your Storage Bins:** Reorganize or shift storage bins to optimize space.

19. **Your Shelves:** Adjust the position of shelves if needed.

20. **Your Broken items:** Inspect any items like jars or cans for cracks or damage.

21. **Your Healthy Foods:** Straighten and organize healthy foods or granola bars.

22. **Your Empty Containers:** Swap out empty, or nearly empty, containers with full ones.

23. **Your Cereal Boxes:** Ensure cereal boxes are properly closed and not stale. Since you can't see inside, check for how much is left.

24. **Your Bottled Goods:** Check bottles of oils or sauces for leaks or damage.

25. **Your Water Supply:** Ensure that any emergency water bottles or supplies are intact.

26. **Trash and Nearly Empty Packages:** Remove nearly empty boxes and packages that clutter your storage space.

27. **Your Overstocks:** Do you have too much of something? Assess and consider rotating stock.

28. **Your Food Storage:** Ensure air-tight containers are properly sealed.

29. **Your Containers:** Make sure labels on any home-made or bulk containers are clear and legible. If you used the fabric boxes mentioned above—label what's in the box.

30. **Your Recipes:** Scan through any recipe cards or books for upcoming meal ideas.

CHAPTER 3

Use Common Sense

Let's pretend you are working in your office. Maybe it's like mine and it's located upstairs in your home. Let's say you have a number of small chores to do that include filing a number of small items.

I am not suggesting that you leave your office for thirty seconds to go downstairs and file one item and then make the trek back upstairs, do another piece of paperwork, and make another trek downstairs. No! Let's use common sense and make one trip to do them all. The 'make the trip and file it' approach applies to one document to be filed and the thirty seconds required to file it instead of delaying a trip and doing something completely unrelated . . . or doing nothing at all.

I'm talking about getting a job done when you have a thirty second period to accomplish it rather than letting things gang up on you.

What I'm trying to say is: don't take thirty seconds from another task to accomplish something that can be done with an otherwise empty thirty-second slot. That is inefficient and will end up costing you time in the long run.

Yes, it might take only thirty seconds to put a book back on the shelf where it belongs, but if you have five books, don't make five trips. Instead, collect all of the books that need to be shelved and make one trip to do this all at once.

On the other hand, if there's only one book or file that needs to be put away and you have a spare thirty seconds, just do it.

Remember, we're trying to use minimal time now to save maximum effort later.

Don't just think about minimal time, think also about minimal spaces . . . like a closet. Here's an easy way to stand in one place and reach a number of items that could use some thirty-second assistance.

Turn the page; and let's see what can be done there:

Thirty Things in Thirty Seconds
You can do in the CLOSET

Doing these kinds of things can make your closet a more pleasant place to use, as well as help you use your time more efficiently. A well-organized closet can be a haven when you can find and manage your clothing and accessories

1. **Your Seasonal things:** Keep winter away from summer items and separate spring and fall, too. Consider using the closet in another room for items out of season.

2. **Your floor:** The floor of your closet can easily become a catch-all spot that quickly becomes cluttered. Hide things on the floor beneath the hanging clothes so they are out of sight yet organized.

3. **Your accessories:** Belts, scarves, ties, and more are easy to misplace or get lost amidst all of the stuff in the closet. Make a place or purchase an organizer for all these things.

4. **Your lights:** You can't imagine how much difference there can be in your closet just by changing a light bulb with a brighter, whiter one. Yes, it really does make a difference, and you'll be able to tell the difference between navy blue items and black ones!

5. **Your hangers:** Align and straighten hangers to keep your clothes organized. Think about plastic hangers of different colors. Use colors to

distinguish one kind of clothing from another: suits, shirts, blouses, pants, dresses, seasons, etc.

6. **Your Shoes:** Place scattered shoes in their proper spot or arrange them neatly.

7. **Your Clothes:** Smooth out any crumpled clothes on shelves or in drawers.

8. **Your Hanging Clothes:** Smooth any hanging clothes that are askew or with noticeable wrinkles.

9. **Your Shelves:** Fix any shelving that's misaligned or in need of a quick tweak.

10. **Your Clutter:** Get rid of any items that don't belong in the closet, like bags or miscellaneous objects that you are just storing.

11. **Your Other Items:** Move items around to make frequently used clothes or accessories more accessible. If you used the suggestion for assorted colors of hangers, now arrange each color into its own groups.

12. **Your Damaged Items:** Look for any signs of damage on clothes, like tears or stains.

13. **Your Drawer Contents:** Organize or adjust the contents of any drawers in the closet.

14. **Your Shelves:** Use a cloth to quickly wipe down any shelves if they've gathered dust.

15. **Your Seasonal Items:** Briefly check seasonal items to ensure they're stored properly.

16. **Your Laundry:** Identify and remove any dirty clothes or laundry items.

17. **Your Loose Clothing and Miscellaneous Items:** Hang up any clothes or items that are draped over furniture or shelves.

18. **Your Closet Fresheners:** Replace/refresh air fresheners or deodorizers in the closet.

19. **Your Floor Space:** Remove any items from the closet floor that might be cluttering the space.

20. **Your Clothing Rod:** Check if the clothing rod needs adjustment in height or if items are getting stuck when you slide the hanger. Is the rod secure and not sagging?

21. **Your Jewelry:** Put jewelry or accessories in their designated spots or put them away in a good storage spot.

22. **Your Towels:** If you store towels in your closet, quickly fold or stack them neatly.

23. **Your Spills:** Look for any spills or stains on closet shelves and clean them up.

24. **Your Old Items:** Remove any old or unused items that you no longer need or use. Get brutal with this one and toss out any items that you previously liked but don't use anymore. Or even better, donate them to a local thrift store.

25. **Your Storage Bins:** Organize any storage bins or containers.

26. **Your cobwebs:** Reach up with paper towel or broom and brush out any cobwebs.

27. **Your Fallen Places:** Scout places where things

can fall and hide behind. Look behind and under things on the top shelf, behind hanging clothes, and behind shoes on the floor.

28. **Your Bags:** Make sure that bags or totes are stored properly and not squished.

29. **Your Vacuum:** If you have a small hand vacuum, give the closet floor a quick sweep.

30. **Your Stored Stuff**: If you used the idea of storing things in fabric boxes, pull one down and glance through its contents just to remind yourself of what's hidden in there.

Again, use common sense. If some of these are not a thirty-second job, you can either stay a little longer or just do thirty seconds now and do another one later.

CHAPTER 4

Where Did the Time Go?

It was not unusual—in fact, it was expected. When we would make our annual trip to see my grandmother, she would always look at us, hug us, and exclaim:

"You've grown up so much since I last saw you! Oh, where did the time go?"

Time has a peculiar way of slipping through our fingers, like grains of sand in an hourglass, steadily marching forward, never pausing to wait for anyone or anything. We often find ourselves caught in the whirlwind of our busy lives, chasing dreams, meeting deadlines, and tending responsibilities.

In the blink of an eye, moments turn into memories. That's when we realize that the people we love, the experiences we cherish, the responsibilities we accept, and the chores we do are quickly fading into the past. Time, in its relentless march, serves as a reminder that we must make the most of every fleeting moment.

Quit saying, "Where did the time go?"

You know where it went. It went bye-bye. It's gone and you either put it to good use or you didn't. If you didn't—it can never be reclaimed. It cannot be regained, redeemed, reused, or replayed. It's just gone.

Time, much like money slipping away through a leak in your bank account, flows relentlessly and inexorably. It's a finite resource that you can either use wisely or allow to slip through your fingers, never to be regained. Every moment that passes is a moment lost, and it's up to us to make the most of the time we have, because the time will come when we don't have it anymore.

Just as management of finances is important, time management is crucial, as well. Procrastination, indecision, and aimless drifting through life day in and day out can result in precious time wasted. Conversely, using your time purposefully, setting goals, and working toward them can lead to a more fulfilling and meaningful life. Time is a non-renewable resource, and once it's gone, it's gone forever.

The metaphor of time as a leak in your bank account serves as a reminder that we must be vigilant in how we spend our days. It's an encouragement to seize opportunities, nurture relationships, and pursue our passions because, in the grand scheme of things, time is the most valuable currency we possess.

The problem is that most of us live and act like our time is in endless supply. But it's not! At least, not yours or mine—it is a finite amount that one day will be gone. It will either have been used or wasted. There will come a day when your stream of time will run dry, like the gas in a car tank it will read "Empty." What then?

Indeed, our time on this Earth is finite. It's one of the few constants in life. Each of us is given a limited amount of time to live, love, learn, and leave our mark on the world. Awareness of this finitude can be a powerful motivator for making the most of our time.

You might be thinking, *you mentioned 'leave your mark on the world,' but my world is pretty much wrapped up in my kitchen. What can I do there?*

Did I hear you ask, "What can I do in thirty seconds in my little kitchen?" Let's see if we can list thirty things in thirty seconds there . . .

Thirty Things in Thirty Seconds
You can do in the KITCHEN

These tasks can help keep your kitchen running smoothly and ensure everything is in its place!

1. **Service Your Silverware:** Organize the cutlery drawer.

2. **Keep Your Towels in Order:** Organize your drawer for dishtowels.

3. **Tackle 'that' Drawer:** Declutter the 'catch-all' (miscellaneous or junk) drawer.

4. **Untangle Cords:** Put the appliance cords with the proper appliance and use old paper towel tubes to store cords.

5. **Putter with Pots:** Organize just one stack of pots and pans.

6. **Keep Puttering:** Do it again with another stack (at another time).

7. **Still Keep Puttering:** Repeat until all are in order (but only at thirty seconds each time).

8. **Clear Surfaces:** Wipe the crumbs and gunk off the stovetop and countertop.

9. **Rinse dishes:** (Too many for a half minute? Do some of them and do the others on another commercial break. Use the unused thirty-second packages of time.

10. **Dry Dishes:** It only takes a moment to keep your dishes spot-free.

11. **Load the Dishwasher:** You'll thank yourself later when you have a clean sink.

12. **Fill the Kettle:** Start filling the kettle with water for your next cup of tea or coffee.

13. **Check the Fridge:** Take a brief glance inside the fridge to see if anything needs to be used soon or is running low.

14. **Refrigerate Leftovers:** Put leftover food into a container and place it in the fridge.

15. **Organize Utensils:** Quickly put away any misplaced kitchen utensils or tools.

16. **Clear Counter:** Quickly remove any items or clutter from your kitchen counters.

17. **Wipe Down Surfaces:** Use a cloth or disinfecting wipe to clean a small area of the counter or stovetop.

18. **Organize Utensils:** Arrange kitchen utensils or gadgets neatly in their designated spots.

19. **Check Appliances:** Make sure appliances like the toaster or coffee maker are turned off.

20. **Clean Sink:** Rinse out the sink or quickly wipe down the sink area.

21. **Straighten Spice Rack:** Quickly arrange spice jars or bottles so they're easy to find.

22. **Inspect Dish Drainer:** Quickly check if the dish drainer needs to be emptied or cleaned.

23. **Clean Microwave:** Wipe down the microwave door or clean any spills inside.

24. **Check Paper Towels:** Ensure you have enough paper towels and replace the roll if needed.

25. **Clear Table:** Remove any items from the dining table or kitchen table.

26. **Refresh Kitchen Towels:** Replace or straighten kitchen towels that are hanging or on the counter.

27. **Check Trash Can:** Ensure the trash can is not overflowing and replace the liner if necessary.

28. **Check Dish Soap:** Ensure you have enough dish soap and replace the bottle if needed.

29. **Prepare Coffee Maker:** Set up the coffee maker for your next cup of coffee or tea.

30. **Check Oven:** Ensure the oven is clean or quickly remove any visible crumbs or spills.

CHAPTER 5

The Lifetime Countdown Watch

When I was forty-eight years old, I asked God to give me twenty-five more years of effective service for Him. There was no voice of agreement from heaven and no contract was signed, but I live with a mark on the date twenty-five years from the time I made that prayer.

Twenty-five years from when I was forty-eight means I will be seventy-three when this covenant is complete. A few Christmases ago, my wife asked me what I wanted as a gift. I suggested a watch I can set for my seventy-third birthday, and it will tell me how much time I have left. I'm now seventy-two-plus years old and as I type this sentence, that watch tells me I have:

Nine months + twenty-three days + thirteen hours
and eleven minutes until that time.
I live with that watch daily.
I look at that watch daily.
I measure my life by that watch daily.
I choose the activities of my life by that watch daily.

The concept of knowing the exact amount of time you have left is both intriguing and sobering. While we don't have the ability to predict our lifespan with such precision, the idea of having approximately nine months, twenty-three days, thirteen hours, and now ten minutes left can serve as a powerful reminder to use your time wisely and make the most of every moment.

Recognizing the finite nature of time can lead to a greater appreciation for life's moments, a deeper sense of purpose, and a heightened awareness of what truly matters. It encourages us to prioritize our goals, nurture our relationships, and focus on the things that bring us joy and fulfillment. It reminds us that time is a precious resource not to be squandered, but to be cherished and used wisely.

Okay, so maybe you don't have a 'lifetime countdown watch.' You didn't offer an agreement with God on the length of your life. What does this mean to you?

You and I Are Alike in Many Ways

Consider these thoughts:

- Just like me, you have a limited span of time until the end of your life.
- Just like me, every moment, second, minute, and hour of your time is being spent.
- Just like me, you are responsible for choosing how, when, and where it is spent.
- Just like me, you will either use or waste each moment of each day of every year left.

Will you have used it wisely, at your own discretion, and for your chosen goals? Or will it just leak profusely, leaving you to wonder where it all went?

As I mentioned, there was no voice from heaven and no contract signed, but I choose to live my life as if there was. God is free to take me before those twenty-five years are up ... or, on that day, or by His grace, I could live another twenty or thirty years.

If He takes me early, I have no complaints. I will have chosen how to live and how to spend the time He gave me. If He takes me on that day, I have no complaints. It was what I willingly asked for.

If, by His grace, I live longer, I'll have no complaints. I'll buy another watch that will keep track of the days I will be blessed to receive as a gift from Him. That watch will be my daily reminder of all the gratitude I can express to Him.

Each day until then and after then, I choose how to live it.

Each day I will be grateful and decide how to spend my moments, my minutes, my hours, days, weeks, years ... my life.

Remember that while knowing the exact time of your life's end may be impossible, the intent to live each day with purpose and intention can make a profound difference in your life and in the quality of that life. Regardless of the time you have left, using it wisely to create a fulfilling and meaningful life is a goal worth pursuing.

And your time is ticking—right now, as you read this. It's ticking even as you are deciding whether to redeem your time or not.

Where are you right now? If you're a guy, maybe you have things to do in the garage ... or maybe you just enjoy being there. Are there things you can do to 'redeem the time' in that space? Turn the page to see if there are at least thirty things you can do in thirty seconds in your garage!

Thirty Things in Thirty Seconds
You can do in the GARAGE

These quick action items can help keep your garage organized, functional, safe, and ready for use. And, once more, some may require more than thirty seconds, so you can either work a little longer or come back for another thirty-second investment of your time.

1. **Organize Tools:** Quickly put away a few tools or equipment that are out of place.

2. **Check for Clutter:** Scan the garage for any obvious clutter or items that need to be tidied up. Put away what you failed to put away before.

3. **Inspect Tires:** Take a moment to check the air pressure or general condition of your vehicle's tires.

4. **Wipe Down Surfaces:** Use a cloth or paper towel to clean a small area of dust or spills on shelves or workbenches.

5. **Review Inventory:** Check if you need to restock essentials like cleaning supplies or gardening tools.

6. **Dispose of Trash:** Throw away any trash or recyclables that might have accumulated. Yes, even the trash and unused things in your car.

7. **Check Lighting:** Ensure that any lights or bulbs are working properly and replace any that are out.

8. **Secure Loose Items:** Quickly fasten or store any items that may be prone to falling or shifting.

9. **Update a To-Do List:** Jot down any tasks or projects you need to tackle in the garage.

10. **Look for Missing Items:** Briefly scan for any items that you need but can't find.

11. **Organize Tools:** Quickly put away any tools that are out of place.

12. **Sort Recycling:** Quickly sort and place recyclable items into their proper bin.

13. **Inspect Equipment:** Briefly check the condition of garden equipment or power tools.

14. **Tidy Shelves:** Arrange or straighten items on shelves for better organization.

15. **Inspect for Leaks:** Look for any signs of leaks or spills on the floor.

16. **Check Battery Levels:** If you have battery-operated tools, check their charge levels.

17. **Organize Storage Bins:** Quickly arrange or label storage bins for easier access.

18. **Fold Extension Cords:** Neatly fold or coil any extension cords to prevent tangling.

19. **Inspect for Pests:** Look for signs of pests or rodents and address any immediate concerns.

20. **Clean a Small Area:** Quickly sweep or clean a small section of the garage floor.

21. **Check Gas Levels:** For equipment like lawnmowers or leaf blowers, check the gas levels.

22. **Organize Fasteners:** Arrange screws, nails, and other fasteners in their designated containers.

23. **Check Lights:** Ensure all garage lights are working properly.

24. **Tidy Workbench:** Quickly straighten up any clutter on your workbench or table.

25. **Inspect Vehicle:** Take a brief look at your vehicle's exterior for any visible issues.

26. **Check Fire Extinguisher:** Ensure the fire extinguisher is in place and up to date.

27. **Organize Paint Supplies:** Arrange paint cans and brushes neatly if you have them stored.

28. **Adjust Garden Tools:** Quickly sharpen or adjust garden tools if needed.

29. **Verify Security:** Ensure that windows and doors are securely locked or closed.

30. **Clean Small Spills:** Quickly mop up any small spills or stains on the garage floor.

CHAPTER 6

What You Can and Can't Do with Time

The difficult we do immediately.
The impossible takes a little longer.

Understanding what you can and can't do with time emphasizes the significance of making intentional choices and prioritizing activities that align with your values and goals. Time management and mindful living become essential in optimizing the use of this finite resource.

How you use and spend your time is your choice. And, in choosing, the results and consequences of those choices are also yours. Time is a fundamental aspect of our existence, and you need to understand what can and cannot be done with it.

You have the power to make choices about how you allocate and utilize the time you have. **You**, not anyone else.

As I've said, time is a finite, invaluable, and non-renewable resource. Using time wisely can vary greatly from person to person because it's subjective and deeply personal. It might involve pursuing passions, building meaningful relationships, learning new skills, or contributing to causes you care about. Recognizing the distinction between these uses of time can lead to more intentional and fulfilling living.

What You Can't Do:

- You can't **save** time—not in the sense of packing it up and using it later. The time you have now, you must use it now . . . not later.
- You can't **buy** time—no one has a supply from which you can barter or buy.
- You can't **kill** time—it is neither alive nor dead.
- You can't **make** time—it is neither created nor destroyed
- You can't **slow** time—it flows continuously, constantly, and uninterrupted.
- You can't **stop** time—you can pause your TV, but not your life.
- You can't **reverse** time—it only flows in one direction from the now into the past
- You can't **change** the past—its time has passed and there is no going back.

What You Can Do:

- You can **bide** your time—to wait patiently until a more ideal moment or situation reveals itself.
- You can **use time wisely**—this means making deliberate choices about how you invest your time in activities that align with your goals, values, and personal growth.
- You can **use time effectively**—that is, you produce maximum outcome, but do so using minimum effort.

○ You can **use time productively**—to achieve greatest and highest results.

○ You can **plan time for the future**—but you can't promise it.

○ You can **create memories** with time—by choosing activities that make a lasting impression.

○ You can use time to **learn and grow**—it is always beneficial to learn new things.

○ You can use time to **connect with others**—at the end of your life, the time you have spent with people you love will be what matters most.

○ You can use time to **reflect, evolve, and better yourself**—there is always room for improvement.

○ You can **waste time**—when you fritter it away on unproductive or meaningless activities, but you are essentially squandering this precious resource. Time wasted is time that can never be recovered.

○ You can **spend time**—like money, you can exchange your time for other things. You "spend" time on necessary activities like work, chores, and daily routines. These are essential aspects of life, but they may not always bring immediate personal fulfillment.

Only you have the power to make choices about how you allocate and utilize the time you have. **You,** not anyone else.

Thirty Things in Thirty Seconds
You can do in the LIVING ROOM

Taking care of these items can help maintain a tidy, comfortable, and welcoming living room environment. And why not? The living room is where most of us actually live and spend most of our time.

1. **Straighten Any Area Rugs:** Make them line up with any wooden planks or tiles on the floor. This can help keep your furniture "lined up" too.

2. **Clean the Floor:** Run a quick vacuum over the carpet to make it neater.

3. **Get Help:** Delegate some of these chores to others.

4. **Remove Pet Hair:** Have a hairy cat or dog? Use strip of duct tape or a roller to pick up hair.

5. **Tidy Up:** Organize, straighten, or dispose of papers and other items scattered around.

6. **Straighten Cushions:** Fluff and arrange couch cushions or throw pillows to make the seating area look tidy and inviting.

7. **Close Drawers and Doors:** Furniture that has drawers and doors look much neater when they are closed and without items hanging out.

8. **Adjust Lighting:** Turn on/off a light or adjust lamps or curtains to change the ambiance.

9. **Check Decor:** Adjust or straighten any decorative items, like picture frames or vases, to ensure they're aligned.

10. **Switch Channels:** Change the TV channel or adjust the volume if the TV is on.

11. **Water Plants:** If you have indoor plants, quickly check to see if they need a bit of water.

12. **Rotate Plants:** Ensure that indoor plants are in proper light or are rotated for even growth.

13. **Organize Cords:** Tidy up any visible cords or cables that might be tangled or out of place.

14. **Reset Remote:** Place the remote control back in its designated spot if it's not already there.

15. **Open or Close Blinds:** Adjust the blinds or curtains to let in more light or block it out.

16. **Clear Coffee Table:** Remove any items that don't belong or wipe down the coffee table.

17. **Organize Magazines:** Quickly arrange or stack magazines neatly on the coffee table or a side table. Fan them out to show what's underneath rather than just stacking them up in a single file.

18. **Fold Blankets:** Neatly fold or drape any throw blankets over the back of the couch.

19. **Check for Dust:** Use a quick swipe to check for and remove dust from visible surfaces.

20. **Adjust Furniture:** Ensure that furniture is aligned properly and not out of place.

21. **Arrange Coasters:** Make sure coasters are in place and not cluttered.

22. **Clean TV Screen:** Wipe down the TV screen or entertainment center if it's dusty.

23. **Reposition Rugs:** Adjust any rugs or mats that may be bunched up or out of place.

24. **Check Pillows:** Make sure decorative pillows are evenly spaced and look tidy.

25. **Organize Side Tables:** Straighten up items on side tables or end tables.

26. **Check Heating/Cooling:** Adjust the thermostat or heating/cooling settings if needed.

27. **Clear Entryway:** Quickly tidy up any items in the entryway or near the front door.

28. **Refresh Room Scents:** Use a room spray or diffuser to refresh the living room's scent.

29. **Pick Up Shoes:** Gather and place any stray shoes or slippers back in their designated spot.

30. **Check for Stains:** Look for any visible stains on the couch or carpet and address them.

31. **BONUS—Inspect Fireplaces:** Ensure the fireplace area is clean and free of debris.

32. **BONUS—Arrange Books:** Quickly straighten or stack books on shelves or tables.

33. **BONUS—Replace Light Bulbs:** If a light is out, replace the bulb if you have a spare handy.

34. **BONUS—Dust Ceiling Fan:** That fan collects a lot of dust on the upper side of the blades. It's a great place for dirt to hide and an important place to clean.

35. **BONUS—Wipe Down the Top of Doorways:** This is another place that dust and dirt love to hide. One damp cloth and thirty seconds and all door frames can be done.

CHAPTER 7

You Can't MAKE Time, But You Can FIND It

I used to live on the beach, and it wasn't unusual to find a beachcomber with a metal detector looking for lost treasures. He was not in the business of "making" treasures . . . he was finding them. In a similar way, you can't 'make time,' you can only find what might have been lost if you had not been looking for it. But if you're looking for small moments in which you can accomplish meaningful things, you can find it.

In other words, you can't MAKE time, but you can FIND it. And, as you know, I've discovered that it often comes in packages of thirty-second increments at a time. So, these short bursts do add up . . . and you can be the richer for using them.

Earlier today, I was filing a horde of papers away into various file folders. I had hanging files, a label maker, file folders, important car papers, and receipts for things and services. I had drawers opened and spent quite a while looking in them trying to place things in their proper location.

Why? Because I wanted everything to be organized.

Why? Because, being organized, I can manage my time better when I need to find something.

Did all those files and papers show up at once? No. When I came across one, I would set it aside and stack it with others that were already saved for the same purpose. Then, when they accumulated to a sizeable stack, I got my workspace organized with the required file folders, marker pens, stapler, and more, and I went to work making a home for each orphaned piece of paper.

It took quite a while but eventually the job was done, and I felt I had accomplished something significant. But that's when I also realized I could have filed each of those pieces of paper in less than thirty seconds when it was first needed, and it would never have become this labor-intensive, time-consuming task. Instead, I had saved them up and made a full morning project out of the mess. The time I was spending on this project would not have even been necessary if I had followed my dad's advice. He used to tell me, "Handle each piece of paper only once."

When you have a piece of paper, make a decision about it and put it in its proper place. I never saw the wisdom in that until I found myself committing hari-kari suicide by papercuts. Once I got the hang of the "thirty-second rule," I saw the wisdom of it.

So, what did I do? I singled out several papers and files, put them in a stack, and timed myself as I went about filing them as if they were all individually being processed. Sure enough, I found that while I had put off this task, each one could have been handled, processed, and finalized in less than thirty seconds. If only I'd done it that way when I first handled it.

Thirty seconds wasn't too long to ask someone to wait, to hold dinner, to pause the TV... and if I'd done that previously, I wouldn't have had to reserve a 'filing frenzy morning' to get the job done.

Throughout this book, I hope to show you how you can 'find the time' by 'taking the time' and not 'making the time' by teaching you how to use the thirty-second rule.

Understand this: we're not just talking about where you are, because the rule applies to what you have, as well. Let's suppose for a moment that you left a screwdriver out the last time you were working on a project. You're not in any particular room, but you have a screwdriver ... and thirty seconds. Is there something you can do with that tool in such a short time?

Let's turn the page and see...

Thirty Things in Thirty Seconds
You can do WITH A SCREWDRIVER

With just a bit of skill and the right screwdriver, you can tackle a lot of small repair and maintenance tasks quickly!

1. **Fix Furniture:** Tighten a screw in a piece of furniture.

2. **Get Loose:** Loosen a screw that has become too tight.

3. **Power Up the Remote:** Remove a battery cover from a remote control.

4. **Door Dash:** Adjust a door handle or knob.

5. **Brighten Up the Room:** Change a light switch cover plate.

6. **Fix a Cabinet:** Tighten a cabinet hinge.

7. **Don't Get Shocked:** Install a new outlet cover plate.

8. **Protect Your Head:** Fix a loose light fixture.

9. **Protect Your Work:** Tighten screws on a laptop or computer.

10. **Access Wires:** Remove a switch plate to access wiring.

11. **Get it Together:** Assemble a piece of flat-pack furniture.

12. **Fix a Drawer:** Secure a loose drawer pull.

13. **Improve a Door:** Adjust the tension on a door closer.

14. **Hang a Picture:** Install a wall hook or picture hanger.

15. **Seriously, Don't Get Shocked:** Remove a cover from an electrical box.

16. **Get a Handle of the Situation:** Fix a loose handle on a door.

17. **Safety First:** Replace the battery in a smoke detector.

18. **Ride Safely:** Tighten screws on a bicycle or bike accessory.

19. **Change Batteries:** Remove a small cover from a gadget or appliance.

20. **See the Light:** Adjust the screws on a pair of eyeglasses.

21. **Sit Tight:** Reattach a loose chair leg.

22. **Entertain Yourshelf:** Install a new shelf bracket.

23. **Switch it Up:** Fix a loose switch on an appliance.

24. **The Key to Life:** Install a keyhole cover or decorative plate.

25. **Really! Don't Get Shocked:** Secure a loose electrical outlet.

26. **Play Around:** Remove a screw from a toy.

27. **Hang Tight:** Adjust a curtain rod bracket.

28. **Keep it on the Wall:** Tighten screws on a picture frame.

29. **Decisive Devices:** Remove a small access panel on a device.

30. **Protect the Walls:** Replace a screw in a door strike plate.

CHAPTER 8

The "Thirty Second Rule"

When I was a kid, we often used the five-second rule about food that dropped onto the table or floor. If it was something we really wanted (the last of the butterscotch lifesavers) even if it landed in the dirt, we'd brush it off and claim the five-second rule! What was that? As long as it didn't remain "contaminated" for longer than five seconds, we could reclaim it and absolve it of all its pollution!

In a similar way, you can learn to use the thirty-second rule and use it to your advantage. This is where you find the time. The rule goes like this:

If you can do this (job, task, event) in thirty seconds—do it!

Do it **NOW**!

Don't put it off. Reclaim the longer time it would take to do it later and just do it now!

As stated previously, life is full of tasks that can be monstrous or miniscule. Learn the difference. What makes the difference? The amount of time required to bring about a satisfactory solution to each effort.

You will be amazed as to how so many of life's little tasks can be broken down and fit into this incredibly small amount of time! No, seriously. I've been timing my many varied daily tasks, and I've noted those that I conveniently delay doing because I don't want to take the time to do it now (and it's staggering to realize how many of those things that I procrastinated) could have been done within the bounds of the thirty second rule!

Let me give you a sample to prove my point:

> I live in a two-story house. My office is located in a bedroom overlooking the front yard. When I hear the mail being delivered, I postpone retrieving it because it takes time to get out of my chair and walk through my office, to and down the stairs, across the hall, out the front door, across the front yard, and to the mailbox. Why would I stop what I'm doing for the length of time it takes to do all that?

> **Then I timed it: thirty seconds!**

> I decided that I would put off the job of hanging a 'Welcome' sign by the front door until Saturday. I just didn't want the involved process of getting from the front porch to the garage and find my screwdriver.

> **Then, I timed it: thirty seconds!**

I needed some tools for my pool, but they were out back in the storage shed. I decided it was too far and too hot for such a small need. I'd put it off until I was going to go out there for something else. That sounded like a time-saver, but actually, it was just prolonged procrastination.

So, I timed the trip to the shed, and you guessed it: thirty seconds.

My wife and I usually watch television while we eat dinner, and we groan when we have to watch a commercial. It seems as though the commercials get longer (and maybe they do), but we don't budge from our seats because the show might continue at any moment. The dirty dishes? Oh, those can wait. Why? Because they take too long? Really? To pick it up, walk to the kitchen, and rinse it?

You know what's coming . . . I timed it: thirty seconds

Knowing this, I may never have to watch another commercial again. You can do that too! If you need to, every time a commercial comes on your television, surprise yourself with what you can get done before your show begins again.

What I'm discovering is that much of life can be accomplished in thirty seconds! More than I ever imagined. The more I observe, time, and understand this, I have found it to be revolutionary.

It's not that I get more done, but I get these small tasks done in the time that would have been otherwise wasted or misspent at best. I simply learned to 'move' my task from some unspecified future time to the immediate moment and filled an otherwise unused, unreserved (read 'spent and wasted') period that freed up that future time for other things. So, in that respect, I can get more done in the future because I didn't put off into the future what I could do now . . . in thirty seconds.

Someone might be thinking, *"That might work if I am home, but I'm in my car waiting in the parking lot for my wife to exit Walmart! There's nothing I can do worthwhile if I'm stuck in my car!"*

Really? Hmmm . . . let's see if we can think of thirty things. Read on . . .

Thirty Things in Thirty Seconds
You can do IN YOUR CAR

These tasks can help ensure your car is clean, organized, and in good condition.

1. **Adjust Seat Position:** Adjust your seat for better comfort or visibility.

2. **Clean Dashboard:** Wipe down the dashboard to remove dust or fingerprints. Think about keeping Armor All wipes under your seat for times like this.

3. **Check Mirrors:** Adjust your rearview and side mirrors for optimal visibility. Has somebody else been driving your car? They probably changed your settings.

4. **Organize Glove Box:** Quickly sort and arrange items in your glove box. Get rid of the junk that tends to collect there. Put back any emergency tools you may need.

6. **Check Tire Pressure:** Use a tire pressure gauge to quickly check your tire pressure. Keep one of those in your glove box.

7. **Clean Windshield:** Use a windshield cleaner or wipe to clear any smudges or dirt. Think about keeping some window cleaner spray in the trunk of the car.

8. **Check Fuel Level:** Look at your fuel gauge to see if you need to refuel soon. Well, that one only took about two seconds, right? Go ahead and do another task.

9. **Adjust Temperature:** Set or adjust the climate control to a comfortable temperature. And perhaps that one took another five seconds? That still gives you twenty more to check some other tasks.

10. **Inspect Lights:** Quickly check that all exterior lights (headlights, turn signals, brake lights) are functioning. Yes, you might have to get outside the car for this one, but it can still be done quickly

11. **Organize Console:** Tidy up the center console, ensuring that items are neatly arranged. Think about keeping a plastic bag nearby to put 'alien' items in (your wife's lipstick? Your husband's golf tee? The used apple sauce squeeze bag your kids begged for?)

12. **Check Fluids:** Check the levels of essential fluids like oil, coolant, and windshield washer fluid.

13. **Clean Seats:** Use a vacuum or cloth to quickly remove crumbs or small debris from the seats.

14. **Check Battery:** Ensure that your car battery is secure and that the terminals are clean.

15. **Inspect Wipers:** Make sure windshield wipers are in good condition and functioning properly. Spray the windshield and note any marks, streaks, or missed spots when the wipers function.

16. **Check Documents:** Verify that your registration and insurance documents are in the glove box. You never know when an officer of the law will ask for them.

17. **Clear Rearview Mirror:** Wipe or clean the rearview mirror to ensure that it's free of smudges. Not all the marks are from your spouse's breath or fingers. The plastic in your car allows fumes that can dull the sharp image of your mirrors and windshield.

18. **Organize Trunk:** Quickly arrange or tidy up items in the trunk. I keep a plastic shoebox and a bag of plastic bags where the spare tire goes.

19. **Adjust Radio:** Set or adjust the radio, media player, and GPS to your preferred station, playlist, and location.

20. **Check Seatbelts:** Ensure that all seatbelts are functioning properly and not tangled. Sometimes the older ones get 'stuck.'

21. **Inspect Air Filter:** Check the air filter if it's easily accessible.

22. **Refresh Air Freshener:** Replace or adjust the air freshener if needed.

23. **Check Window Condition:** Ensure that windows are clear and free from cracks or damage.

24. **Secure Loose Items:** Secure any loose items that might be rolling around.

25. **Review GPS Settings:** Check or update your GPS navigation settings if you're planning a route.

26. **Clean Cup Holders:** Wipe out any spills or crumbs in the cup holders.

27. **Inspect Brakes:** Listen for any unusual noises when applying the brakes.

28. **Check for Warning Lights:** Glance at the dashboard to ensure no warning lights are illuminated.

29. **Adjust Steering Wheel:** Set the steering wheel to a comfortable position.

30. **Verify Emergency Kit:** Ensure that your emergency kit is stocked and easily accessible. I know, it's easy to overlook this one . . . until you need it. Go ahead, check it now.

CHAPTER 9

Time Might Be Infinite . . .
But Not YOURS

Sonic is a fast-food enterprise that used to 'save' time by having all their parking lot food deliveries done by people on roller skates. Did they 'save' time? Well, let's just say time was used more effectively and efficiently so more deliveries could be made within the same amount of time. But they didn't have more time at the end of the day because they 'saved' some . . . no one got to take a box of time home because they 'saved' some while skating.

So, technically, you can't 'save' time and you can't 'make' time; you can only choose to use it or lose it. And the more you use it effectively, the more time you have not used up by that project in the future. This allows you more time later to enjoy, relax, meditate, or put to a more favorable use.

Your time is finite. There's only so much. Just as everyone's bank accounts have various amounts of cash to spend, so is your bank of time. Yes, we all have twenty-four hours every day, but only until your last one, and no one knows when that will be.

There was once a man who asked of God:

> . . . teach us to number our days that we may
> get a heart of wisdom. Psalm 90:12 (ESV)

To make the best use of the time we've been allotted, we need that kind of wisdom. As stated previously: you can't make time or save time. You can only manage it and rearrange the use of it.

So, let's take an account of what you 'might' have.

Assuming (but no guarantee) you live to the age of seventy-two (my age), that's 26,280 days.

Years 0-3 = 1,095 days—you are only 'existing,'
living, breathing, and learning.

Years 4-12 = 3,285 days—you are learning more and playing.

Years 13-20 = 2,920 days—you are a teenager, and those years don't count because you are still trying to discover and create yourself. Hormones, puberty, and self-discovery keep your mind busy, and your future self can change daily.

Years 21-25 = 1,825 days—you are "becoming."

Years 26-72 = 16,790 days—you are who you became.
That's the real you.

16,790 sounds like quite a bit . . . but isn't that all relative?

If you were told you had $16,790 to live on from age twenty-six to seventy-two . . . that's not much.

In fact, that's scary! It comes to roughly only $350/year . . . less than $1/day.

Ouch!

Time is relative, too. Forty-eight years sounds like a lot . . . but only as long as it's in the future. When it has passed, you'll wonder (as my grandmother did) "Where did the time go?"

You will want to use your time effectively and efficiently, getting maximum efficiency with minimum effort.

And that means counting every thirty-second package of time as 'useable' and managing it well.

So, can you REALLY manage time (LOTS of time) like that? Well, let me show you what I learned I could do in thirty seconds. Remember, this is just my time, in my life. Yours may vary.

SECONDS REQUIRED	TRAVEL TO/FROM
20 seconds	Upstairs office to downstairs kitchen
24 seconds	Kitchen to outdoor trashcan
28 seconds	Dining room to shed
15 seconds	Easy chair to master toilet
16 seconds	Easy chair to master closet
23 seconds	Dining table to game room (far end ping pong table)
28 seconds	Game room to tools in garage
30 seconds	Dining room to mailbox with unlocking storm door
17 seconds	Dining room to birdfeeder in back yard

16 seconds	Dining room to file drawers
12 seconds	Dining room to dirty laundry hamper
37 seconds	Dining room to dirty laundry hamper to laundry room
16 seconds	Dining room to garage freezer
25 seconds	Easy chair to back end of garage car (includes putting garage door up)
28 seconds	Car park to shed
35 seconds	Tools to shed
21 seconds	Dining room to hose to plants on patio
29 seconds	Dining room to hose to plants on patio + to garden

Again, your time may vary, but this is the actual time it took me in my home.

Buy yourself a stopwatch and time your life, in your home, at your pace.

Before we go any further, let me say that, yes, I realize that you're probably not on roller skates zipping around parked cars at the local Sonic fast food. You? Maybe you've just walked out to your garden shed. You can tell that your wife, husband, child, or gardener is on the way to meet you there, but they won't arrive for thirty seconds. Can you put that little packet of time to good use?

Turn the page and see if we can come up with a few good ideas . . .

Thirty Things in Thirty Seconds
You can do IN THE GARDEN SHED

Make your gardening experience more efficient. These tasks help keep your garden shed organized and functional.

1. **Keep it Tidy:** Organize bags, jars, cans, aerosols, whatever's in there.

2. **When in Doubt, Throw it Out**: Get rid of anything that is not being used.

3. **Keep it Current:** Toss out anything and everything that is past its expiration date.

4. **Organize Tools:** Quickly put away a few garden tools that are out of place. And while you're there . . .

5. **Check Tool Condition:** Inspect a tool for any damage or wear and tear.

6. **Check Inventory:** Take a glance at your supplies to see if anything is running low.

7. **Wipe Down Surfaces:** Clean a small area of dust or dirt on shelves or workbenches.

8. **Sort Seeds:** Quickly check and sort through your seed packets to ensure they're organized.

9. **Check for Pests:** Look for signs of pests or rodents and address any immediate concerns.

10. **Adjust Shelving:** Rearrange or adjust a shelf to better organize your tools or supplies.

11. **Inspect Pots:** Look over your plant pots for any cracks or damage.

12. **Water Plants:** If you have any plants in the shed, quickly water them.

13. **Secure Cords:** Tidy up any tangled extension cords or hoses.

14. **Replace Light Bulbs:** If a light bulb is burnt out, replace it with a new one.

15. **Dispose of Trash:** Throw away any trash or empty containers that have accumulated.

16. **Check for Leaks:** Inspect for leaks in the shed roof, stored cans, or walls.

17. **Refill Containers:** Refill containers of fertilizers or other garden chemicals if needed.

18. **Tidy Workbench:** Straighten up your workbench and put away any scattered items.

19. **Look for Missing Items:** Search for any tools or supplies that you might be missing.

20. **Adjust Ventilation:** Open or close any vents or windows to adjust airflow.

21. **Clear Pathways:** Remove any items obstructing walkways or access points in the shed.

22. **Inspect Garden Equipment:** Check the condition of larger equipment like lawnmowers or trimmers.

23. **Secure Loose Items:** Fasten or store any loose items that could fall or get damaged.

24. **Check Battery Levels:** If you have battery-operated tools, check their charge levels.

25. Organize Pots and Trays: Arrange plant pots and trays neatly to save space.

26. **Clean Spills:** Mop up any spilled liquids, trash, or soil.

27. **Update a To-Do List:** Note any maintenance tasks or gardening projects you need to address.

28. **Check for Tools in Use:** Retrieve any tools you may have left out from previous use.

29. **Adjust Shed Items:** Make small adjustments to the arrangement of items to improve accessibility.

30. **Inspect for Safety Issues:** Look around for any potential safety hazards like sharp edges, unstable shelving, or tools that might fall.

Know Yourself and Wrestle with Yourself

You can play basketball by yourself.
You can play darts, pool, and bowling by yourself.
You can walk, run, and jump by yourself.
You can climb, golf, and even play catch by yourself.

But wrestling—well, that's different . . . but sometimes it's necessary.

I found myself wrestling with myself in the early hours of the morning. No, it wasn't physical, it was all in my mind. But rest assured it was vigorous!

As I write this, the time is 5:20 a.m. Why am I up this early? My body woke me up because I drank too much juice before going to bed. I chose to stay up because, while going back to sleep might be a good decision, it's a better decision to 'steal' the time for a different purpose. And, of course, I was reminded of a Biblical proverb:

> Go to the ant, O sluggard;
> consider her ways and be wise.
> Without having any chief,
> officer, or ruler,
> she prepares her bread in summer
> and gathers her food in harvest.
> How long will you lie there, O sluggard?
> When will you arise from your sleep?
> A little sleep, a little slumber,
> a little folding of the hands to rest,
> and poverty will come upon you like a robber,
> and want like an armed man.
> Proverbs 6:6-11 (ESV)

I wrestled with the idea of choosing this moment for a better use than what might be an extra hour of sleep. Sometimes, you must choose to use time for a better purpose than what might seem obvious, or even desirable. This is a key to accomplishing your goals and making your days (and life) successful.

Effective time management and goal accomplishment often require making choices that prioritize long-term benefits over short-term gratification. When deciding to stay up and write, it was for a better purpose than sleeping at that moment.

- I was already awake and not too sleepy.
- If I stayed in bed, it would be nice, but I would be thinking about what and when to write what I couldn't get off my mind.
- I knew that this needed to be written sometime today, and if I waited, there was a good chance something else would persuade me to procrastinate.

O I knew everyone else in the household was still asleep, and if they were awake, I could be easily distracted.

O I had no good excuse for procrastinating at this moment, other than the simple joy of getting back to sleep for a little while.

O I weighed the priorities of my choice: the satisfaction of maybe sleeping a little longer versus accomplishing the task of writing one more chapter.

As I looked over this list of the mental gymnastics I was going through, I realized that in the private conversation I was having and the decision process I was going through, there are some key principles to be considered when deciding how to use your time for better purposes.

Here are the principles to consider when making a decision on how to spend your 'extra' time:

1. **Set Clear Goals:** Clearly define your short-term and long-term goals. Knowing what you want to achieve will help you make more informed choices about how you allocate your time.

2. **Prioritize Tasks:** Not all tasks are equal in terms of their importance and impact.

3. **Avoid Distractions:** Identify common distractions in your life: email, social media use, other people, noises, watching/reading the news, the sounds your computer makes for notifications, and more. You must take an honest look at your own proclivities and inclinations and ask yourself, "What easily distracts and besets me?"

4. **Time Blocking:** Allocate specific blocks of time for

different tasks and projects. This helps to ensure that you allocate focused, uninterrupted time to the higher-priority activities.

5. **Say No When Necessary:** It's important to learn to say no to those activities that do not align with your goals. Saying yes to everything can lead to time fragmentation and reduce your productivity.

6. **Delegate and Outsource:** One of my mentors taught me, "Don't be busy doing that which someone else can do when you could be busy doing what only you can do."

If possible, delegate tasks that can be done by others or consider outsourcing non-essential activities to free up your time for more important endeavors.

Ultimately, the key is to be intentional with your time and make choices that align with your goals and values. By doing so, you can use your time more effectively and increase your chances of achieving your objectives.

My wife got up and came into the room a few moments ago. My inclination is to ask her how she slept, if she needs some breakfast, and to discuss our plans for the rest of the day.

So what? The 'so what' is that I can now ask her those things without putting off the writing of this chapter. By choosing to use the quiet time I had rather than the opportunity for just a little more sleep, I accomplished the fulfillment of another chapter of thoughts, and I can still have a morning chat with her.

If I had started with the chat, I know myself well enough that I would have been distracted from getting this chapter down and probably would have put it off for some other time.

What? You're not an early riser? No problem. But have you ever noticed a tool that you left out after completing a task . . . maybe a hammer? You can leave it where it is, or you can put it where it should be . . . or you can use it before you put it away. How would you do that?

Well, maybe it depends on if you can do something useful or helpful with a hammer in thirty seconds. Let's turn the page and see if we can find some . . .

Thirty Things in Thirty Seconds
You can do WITH A HAMMER

A hammer is a very handy tool, but it's usually not nearby when you want it. With that in mind, too many of us tend to put off doing what is needed because we don't want to take the time to get the hammer. But once you get it, there's a lot that can be done!

1. **Drive It:** Drive a nail into a piece of wood.

2. **Remove It:** Remove a nail using the claw side of the hammer.

3. **Tap It:** Tap a small finishing nail gently into place.

4. **Adjust It:** Adjust a loose screw by tapping it with the hammer.

5. **Flatten It:** Flatten a bent nail.

6. **Crack it Open:** Crack open a walnut (if it's a tough one).

7. **Put it in Place:** Lightly tap a metal object into place.

8. **Set It:** Set a drywall anchor by tapping it in.

9. **Get Rid of It:** Remove a small tack from a wall.

10. **Re-Form It:** Shape a piece of metal slightly (e.g., bend it or flatten it).

11. **Straighten It:** Fix a crooked picture frame by adjusting its nails.

12. **Smash It:** Break a small piece of concrete (if it's not too thick).

13. **Fit It:** Tap down a piece of trim so it fits better.

14. **Hook It:** Install a hook or hanger into a wall or piece of wood.

15. **Pinch It:** Pinch a small piece of wood together for gluing.

16. **Align It:** Align a piece of furniture by tapping its joints.

17. **Dig It:** Start a hole in wood or other materials.

18. **Adjust It:** Adjust a door hinge slightly by tapping it.

19. **Flatten It:** Flatten a bent metal strip or bracket.

20. **Secure It:** Secure a cable or wire by tapping a cable staple in.

21. **Tile It:** Tap a tile into place (if it's not yet set).

22. **Eliminate It:** Remove a small piece of plaster from a wall.

23. **Indent It:** Create a small indentation for a screw or nail.

24. **Undent It:** Fix a dent in wood by tapping around the edges.

25. **Caulk It:** Set a bead of caulk into place by tapping it down.

26. **Secure It:** Adjust a fence post by tapping it.

27. **Break It:** Break apart a small piece of debris.

28. **Make It:** Hammer a piece of metal into a makeshift tool.

29. **Mold It:** Shape a piece of clay or other soft material.

30. **Knock It:** Knock loose a small object caught between two surfaces.

CHAPTER 11

The Eisenhower What!?!

President Dwight Eisenhower was a US Army general. He was so astute that he was appointed the supreme allied commander of NATO forces and eventually became the thirty-fourth president of the United States. He carried so much responsibility and had to make so many decisions that he needed a means of calculating the best priorities. He had to consider how to spend his days, hours, minutes, and even his thirty-second time allotments.

To help him do that, he developed the concept behind what would later be called the Eisenhower Matrix. He used it to help him prioritize and deal with the many high-stakes issues he faced . . . and you can use it too.

Those who learn to use their time wisely and redeem that time have often resorted to what is called the "Eisenhower Matrix." It could be helpful for you to take a few moments to develop this kind of thinking for yourself. I know that sounds a little bit 'techie,' but it's an easy-to-understand concept. It goes like this:

Draw a large box and divide it into four connected squares in two-by-two fashion:

Label each square:

- Upper Left: DO—Do it now
- Upper Right: DECIDE—Schedule it for later
- Lower Left: DELEGATE—Assign it to someone else
- Lower Right: ELIMINATE—Just say "no" to it

It looks like this . . . and you decide where to place each of the items on your to-do list in one of those square.

Do Do it now	**Decide** Schedule these items
Delegate Appoint these to someone	**Eliminate** Say "No" to these items

Unbeknownst to me at the time, at 5:20 a.m., I put my to-do items into this matrix.

In the **Do** box was to "Write."
In the **Decide** box was the time with my wife. It could be scheduled for when she woke up (and after her first cup of coffee).
And in the **Eliminate** box was the extra hour of sleep.

Yes, this applies to the thirty-second segments of your life, not just the bigger time decisions. While watching TV at night as a family, our show may be plagued with commercials. I tend to watch them play out and then resume my show. However, I've now noticed that there is often a timer somewhere on the screen showing me how long it takes until my show resumes.

And guess what? That timer shows me how many thirty-second segments of time are available for me to do other things. That's when I now choose to either sit and wait, or to go check the mailbox (twenty-nine seconds to the box), put our nighttime snack dishes in the sink, or do anything else I see that needs to be done.

A proverb from the wisest of men:

**Catch the foxes for us, the little
foxes that spoil the vineyards,
for our vineyards are in blossom.
—Song of Solomon 2:15 (ESV)**

In other words: little foxes spoil the vine, so take care of the small things that could destroy your big things. How can you make the thirty-second rule work for you, even in the bathroom?

Thirty Things in Thirty Seconds
You can do IN YOUR BATHROOM

Taking care of these quick tasks can help keep your bathroom clean, organized, and ready for use!

1. **Think Ahead:** Make sure a new roll of tissue is available and fold the end neatly like they do in an upscale hotel.

2. **Keep it Neat:** Neaten up the area around the sink.

3. **Check the Cupboards:** Organize what's under the sink (don't worry if there's too much for thirty seconds; do it in stages: thirty seconds here and thirty seconds there).

4. **Wipe Down Surfaces:** Clean the sink or countertop with a disinfecting wipe or cloth.

5. **Tidy Towels:** Straighten or hang up any towels that are out of place.

6. **Empty Trash:** Throw away any trash or empty wrappers from the bathroom trash can.

7. **Check Supplies:** Glance at your bathroom supplies like toilet paper or soap to see if anything needs replenishing.

8. **Adjust Shower Curtain:** Make sure the shower curtain is properly closed or adjusted.

9. **Toothbrush Check:** Rinse or organize toothbrushes and toothpaste.

10. **Check Mirror:** Quickly wipe down any smudges or water spots on the mirror.

11. **Refill Soap Dispenser:** If your soap dispenser is running low, add more soap.

12. **Replace Empty Tissues:** Replace an empty tissue box with a new one if needed.

13. **Clean the Toilet Seat:** Quickly wipe down the toilet seat and lid.

14. **Straighten Rugs:** Adjust bathmats or rugs to keep them in place.

15. **Adjust Lighting:** Turn lights on or off or adjust dimmer switches as needed.

16. **Check for Mold:** Look for any signs of mold or mildew and address immediately.

17. **Organize Toiletries:** Tidy up and organize any toiletries or personal items.

18. **Clear Drain:** Make sure the sink or shower drain is clear of any hair or debris.

19. **Inspect Shower Head:** Check the shower head for any buildup or clogs.

20. **Refresh Air:** Open a window or turn on the fan to freshen the air.

21. **Check Bath Products:** Ensure that bath products like shampoo or conditioner are stocked and organized.

22. **Replace Sponges:** If your sponge is worn out, replace it with a new one.

23. **Clear Counter Clutter:** Remove any unnecessary items from the bathroom counter.

24. **Clean Faucet:** Remove fingerprints and water-marks. Wipe down the faucet handle to remove any water spots or grime.

25. **Adjust Bathroom Mat:** Ensure the bathmat is in place and not bunched up or ready to trip someone up.

26. **Check for Leaks:** Quickly inspect for any signs of leaks around the sink or toilet.

27. **Organize Medicine Cabinet:** Straighten items in the medicine cabinet or shelf.

28. **Check Shower Caddy:** Ensure the shower caddy is organized and not overloaded.

29. **Replace Old Razors:** Dispose of old or dull razors and replace with fresh ones, if needed.

30. **Restock Cleaning Supplies:** Check if cleaning supplies are in their place or need restocking.

Ten Important Things That Can Be Done in Thirty Seconds

**"Important things don't have to be big things . . .
they can be small things that accomplish big things."
—Dr. Gerald Robison**

Well, we're coming to the end, and I hope that this book has helped you to reclaim some of your 'wasted' and unused time and maybe even increased your happiness. You really can reduce your stress and live a happier, more fulfilling life by taking thirty seconds here and there to get those pesky chores done that haunt you when you try to relax.

For this final chapter, I wanted to do something different. Thus far, I have shared practical tips on how to get minor chores done in thirty-second intervals, so that they don't pile up and become dreaded all-day cleaning and organizing frenzies. However, while that is helpful to our own mental health, the most important thing in living a happy life is our connections to the people in our lives.

Sometimes, they struggle, too, and what better way to use some of those found moments than to do something that will lift them up? Here are a few suggestions to do just that:

1. **Send or speak a kind or encouraging message:** Wish someone a good day, a happy birthday, anniversary, or even more special, an "I was just thinking of you" comment. Let someone who doesn't think they are special feel special. A small act that pays big dividends.

2. **Say a prayer for someone:** What a great way to use a short amount of time in the service of someone else's well-being!

3. **Focus your attention on someone else:** Can you help them do, think, or plan something they are struggling with?

4. **Show gratitude:** Say a word, send a gift, or take a moment to express gratitude for something or to someone you are thankful for.

5. **Speak a good word to someone usually overlooked:** What about the janitor, service person, toll booth operator, mail server, trash truck operator, or lawn-care person? There are no small people except those who think others are.

6. **Send a card to someone who needs a little sunshine in their lives:** Keep a collection of greeting cards handy and just jot a quick note to someone who needs to be encouraged. Someone in your church, your school, business, family, or

any other person who might benefit from such a small act of kindness.

7. **Pick a flower and give it to someone who no one else will:** Give a flower to an elderly person; someone sitting alone in a park, on a bus, walking on the sidewalk; someone who looks haggard, frenzied, overwhelmed with their children; or someone you notice who may be struggling. Open your eyes as well as your heart and just look—they are all around you.

8. **Pick up someone else's trash and put it where it should be:** Litter is all around us, but those who care and do something about it aren't. Even if no one else cares, it will make you feel good.

9. **Help someone with something bulky and get it in their car:** If you're leaving the grocery store, home improvement store, or big box store, you will probably see at least one person who is struggling to put a large parcel in their trunk, or maybe a harried mother with a crying child trying to soothe them while wrestling with getting all of the groceries in the trunk. Offer to help them in their time of frustration.

10. **Leave a nice handwritten message along with your tip at a restaurant:** Wait staff often get a lot of complaints and negativity while they are working. Why not flip the script and leave a note to let them know that you appreciate them? It takes only a few seconds but can make their entire day brighter.

Have you done any of these at home? For your spouse or kids? Even if it's not 'your job,' can you do something at home that speaks volumes to your significant others? Consider doing these things for someone you would otherwise pass by on the street without even noticing them.

THE TWO MOST IMPORTANT AND PROFITABLE THIRTY SECONDS OF YOUR LIFE

My wife tells me that science has proven the benefits of a meaningful and significant hug every day. They define significant as one that lasts at least twenty seconds in length.

I've tested it with her. Hmmmm ... she may be onto something. That was pretty good! I think I'll try it again. . . (Pause) . . .

Yep! She's right!!

I think that moment can:

- O Calm my pulse
- O Ease my anxiety
- O Clear my mind
- O And it just feels really good

The second immensely important thirty-second package of time is to have a still, quiet moment of gratefulness to God. Like a hug, it also can:

- O Calm my pulse
- O Ease my anxiety
- O Clear my mind
- O And it, too, just feels really good

But it also does two more things:

O It brings peace to my soul and
O Solace to my spirit

Try it. You, too, might like it!

SUGGESTION:

Go to a local sporting goods shop and purchase your own stopwatch. For just a few dollars, you can begin to surprise yourself in how far you can go, and how much you can do, how many things you can scratch from your to-do list - in the time that already exists in your life. So, here's my suggestion:

BUY YOURSELF A STOPWATCH!!

BUY YOURSELF A STOPWATCH!!

BUY YOURSELF A STOPWATCH!!

BUY YOURSELF A STOPWATCH!!

BUY YOURSELF A STOPWATCH!!

Then, involve the rest of your family by asking them to help you time various projects and tasks. I believe you'll find them wanting to make a game of it, and they'll want to do the same thing.

This is a fun way to begin teaching them the same skills for evaluating how they use time in their lives, too. You can begin by asking them questions like:

- O "What would you like to time?"
- O "How fast do you think I can do that?
- O "How fast do you think you can do that?
- O "Let's race and see if we can do this in thirty seconds."

Appendix

Within the coming pages are more lists of Thirty Things You Can Do in Thirty Seconds.

Again, they are not meant to be a checklist, but they can show you that there are a great many things that can be done in the otherwise overlooked and wasted moments of time that you can choose to use or not.

If you choose not to benefit from their use, you also fall victim to the consequences of your choice. Life gets 'backed-up.' You may feel that there's just never enough time! You may find that life just keeps overwhelming you with longer and longer to-do lists.

Again, let me encourage you to not use these suggestions as a checklist, but as an encouragement for you to begin a tour of self-discovery of the many, many things you can do in the small, short, and seemingly inconsequential moments of life.

You can't 'make' time, and you can't 'save' time, but you can manage it.

If you don't, the tasks of those many miniature moments will soon begin to manage and demand your life's time in ways that are less effective and less efficient . . . and less pleasant.

While we know there are sixty seconds in a minute,
And sixty minutes in an hour,
And twenty-four hours in a day,
And 365 days in a year . . .

No one knows how many years, or even days, you will have allotted for your lifetime. Make the most of them. Manage them well.

It's all you get!

Thirty Things in Thirty Seconds
You can do IN YOUR BEDROOM

These quick tasks can help you keep your bedroom organized, comfortable, and inviting. Think about it: you spend approximately eight hours here every day. Make it what you want it to be.

1. **Make the bed:** This is one of the simplest things that can set the direction of your day (or theirs if this isn't your room).

2. **Put clutter away:** This is YOUR space . . . make it livable and desirable.

3. **Clear the 'floor hooks':** Move shoes and left-out clothing and put them where they belong.

4. **Straighten Bed:** Smooth bed pillows, bedspread, and/or sheets; and . . .

5. **Fluff Decoratives:** Fluff and arrange decorative pillows and flowers.

6. **Adjust Lighting:** Turn off or dim lights, or open blinds to let in natural light.

7. **Tidy Nightstand:** Organize or clear any items on your nightstand, like books or chargers.

8. **Check Alarm Clock:** Ensure your alarm clock is set correctly or adjust the time.

9. **Check Under the Bed:** Peek under the bed to make sure there's no visible clutter or dust (or monsters if it's a child's room).

10. **Fold Clothes:** Quickly fold any clothes that might be draped over a chair or bed.

11. **Organize Drawers:** Adjust or straighten the items in your bedside drawers.

12. **Clear Surfaces:** Wipe down or clear off any surfaces that have collected dust or clutter.

13. **Refresh Air:** Open a window for a few seconds or turn on a fan for a quick freshen-up.

14. **Adjust Temperature:** Adjust the thermostat or open/close a window to set a comfortable temperature.

15. **Straighten Rug:** Adjust or straighten any rugs or mats on the floor.

16. **Organize Books:** Straighten any books or magazines on a nightstand or shelf.

17. **Dust Surfaces:** Don't forget the "other" places often overlooked: bed knobs and crevices, drawer handles and decorative carving, top of the mirror, the back of the TV. Look for the usually forgotten places.

18. **Arrange Shoes:** Organize any shoes that might be scattered around.

19. **Adjust Curtains:** Open or close curtains or blinds to control light and privacy.

20. **Check for Laundry:** If you see any dirty laundry, toss it in a hamper.

21. **Reset Furniture:** Adjust any furniture or decorative items that may have shifted.

22. **Check Jewelry:** Put away or organize any jewelry that might be left out in the open.

23. **Organize Remotes:** Arrange or place any TV remotes or other gadgets in their designated spots.

24. **Change Pillowcases:** If needed, replace pillowcases with fresh ones.

25. **Check the Bed:** Reset the bed skirt and length of bedspread so they are even and well-adjusted.

26. **Inspect Walls:** Look for any scuffs or marks on the walls and quickly wipe them if needed.

27. **Check Bedside Lamp:** Ensure the bedside lamp is working and properly positioned.

28. **Organize Cords:** Tidy up any visible cords or cables around your bed or nightstand.

29. **Refresh Bedding:** Adjust or shake out the bedding to remove wrinkles.

30. **Set Out Fresh Towels:** If you keep extra towels in the bedroom, fold and set them out neatly.

Thirty Things in Thirty Seconds
You can do with a TAPE GUN

A tape gun is a handy tool for quick fixes and packaging tasks, making it versatile for a wide range of uses!

1.   **Seal a cardboard box** for shipping or storage.

2.   **Reinforce a package** by adding extra tape to the seams.

3.   **Attach a shipping label** to a package.

4.   **Wrap a gift** quickly by taping down the wrapping paper.

5.   **Seal a bag of food** or other items.

6.   **Create a makeshift label** on a box or container.

7.   **Fix a loose piece of trim** temporarily.

8.   **Secure a roll of bubble wrap** around fragile items.

9.   **Patch a small tear** in a piece of paper or plastic.

10. **Mount a poster** on a wall or board.

11. **Tape down wires** to keep them organized.

12. **Wrap a bundle of papers** together.

13. **Secure a small object** inside a package.

14. **Attach a note or card** to a gift or package.

15. **Create a temporary repair** on a torn document.

16. **Seal an envelope** quickly.

17. **Fix a loose or peeling edge** on a piece of laminate.

18. **Secure an item** to a display board.

19. **Create a temporary label** for a storage container.

20. **Hold two objects together** for a quick fix.

21. **Wrap up a set of tools** or equipment for storage.

22. **Seal a small crack** or hole in packaging.

23. **Attach a promotional flyer** to a door or bulletin board.

24. **Bundle up cables** or cords for neat storage.

25. **Create a makeshift handle** on a bag or box.

26. **Fix a loose part** on a piece of furniture.

27. **Secure a piece of plastic sheeting** temporarily.

28. **Attach a photo** to a display board.

29. **Wrap up a small gift** or token.

30. **Fix a tear** in a book cover.

Thirty Things in Thirty Seconds
You can do with a PLASTIC BAG

Plastic bags are versatile and handy for a multitude of quick tasks. And most of us have hundreds of them lurking around.

1. **Pack a lunch** or snacks for the day.

2. **Wrap up trash** for easy disposal.

3. **Protect items** from moisture or dirt.

4. **Carry groceries** or other small items.

5. **Organize small items** like craft supplies or screws.

6. **Cover a plant pot** to prevent soil from spilling.

7. **Keep shoes clean** when packing them.

8. **Wrap a gift** for a quick and easy presentation.

9. **Store leftovers** in the fridge.

10. **Keep electronics** like cables and chargers together.

11. **Protect documents** or papers from water damage.

12. **Use as a temporary glove** for handling messy tasks.

13. **Create a makeshift ice pack** by filling it with ice.

14. **Collect and dispose** of pet waste.

15. **Seal up** opened food packages.

16. **Pack small items** for travel or storage.

17. **Use as a funnel** for pouring liquids.

18. **Keep car essentials** like maps or tools organized.

19. **Cover a bowl** to let dough rise or keep food warm.

20. **Store seasonal decorations** for easy access.

21. **Wrap a wet umbrella** to keep other items dry.

22. **Protect items in a moving box**.

23. **Create a temporary rain cover** for electronics.

24. **Carry a small amount of sand** or dirt.

25. **Wrap a broken item** to prevent further damage.

26. **Protect your hands** while handling chemicals or paints.

27. **Organize your backpack** or handbag.

28. **Use as a makeshift pouch** for carrying loose items.

29. **Protect a book** from rain or spills.

30. **Store emergency supplies** like first aid items.

Thirty Things in Thirty Seconds
You can do with a VACUUM

Vacuum cleaners are incredibly efficient for quick clean-ups and targeted tasks!

1. **Vacuum a small area** of carpet.

2. **Remove crumbs** from a kitchen counter.

3. **Clean a single spot** on the floor.

4. **Pick up pet hair** from a couch or chair.

5. **Suck up dust** from a table or shelf.

6. **Vacuum a small rug** or mat.

7. **Clean a car interior** or a small section of it.

8. **Remove debris** from a floor or hallway.

9. **Vacuum out a small drawer** or cabinet.

10. **Clean the upholstery** on a chair or sofa.

11. **Pick up dirt** around a high-traffic entryway.

12. **Vacuum a few steps** on a staircase.

13. **Clear out the crumbs** from a toaster tray.

14. **Suck up spider webs** from a corner.

15. **Clean a small area** of hardwood floors.

16. **Vacuum dust** from a baseboard.

17. **Remove small particles** from a carpeted area.

18. **Clean a small pile of sawdust** from a workbench.

19. **Vacuum the vents** of a heating or cooling unit.

20. **Pick up sand or dirt** from a porch or entryway.

21. **Clean under furniture** that has accessible spaces.

22. **Vacuum up small craft supplies** like glitter.

23. **Remove debris** from a pet bed or blanket.

24. **Clean a small section of the ceiling** if accessible.

25. **Pick up crumbs** from a dining table.

26. **Vacuum the dust** from electronic equipment like a TV.

27. **Remove loose dirt** from a shoe rack.

28. **Clean out** a small closet.

29. **Suck up spilled dry ingredients** in the kitchen.

30. **Clean out a drawer** or a small container.

Thirty Things in Thirty Seconds
You can do with a GARDEN HOSE

A garden hose is incredibly versatile for various quick tasks in and around the yard!

1. **Water a small section** of your garden.

2. **Wash off garden tools** after use.

3. **Clean a driveway** or pathway.

4. **Water your** potted plants.

5. **Fill** a birdbath.

6. **Wash your car** quickly.

7. **Rinse off** patio furniture.

8. **Clean** a small outdoor rug.

9. **Water your lawn** in a specific area.

10. **Rinse leaves and debris** off sidewalks.

11. **Clean** your outdoor grill.

12. **Cool down pets** on a hot day.

13. **Water** freshly planted seeds.

14. **Fill** up a kiddie pool.

15. **Clean** a bicycle.

16. **Water** hanging baskets.

17. **Rinse off** outdoor play equipment.

18. **Remove mud** from outdoor surfaces.

19. **Wash down a garden shed** or outdoor structure.

20. **Water** a small vegetable patch.

21. **Fill a large bucket** for other uses.

22. **Rinse off** garden produce.

23. **Clean a window** on the exterior of your house.

24. **Water freshly seeded areas** of your lawn.

25. **Wet down** a compost pile.

26. **Flush out** a rain barrel.

27. **Water herbs** in a small herb garden.

28. **Clean up** after a barbecue.

29. **Rinse off children's toys** left outside.

30. **Water newly** planted shrubs.

Thirty Things in Thirty Seconds
You can do with a SHOVEL

A shovel is a versatile tool that can be used for numerous quick tasks around the yard or garden!

1. **Dig a small hole** for planting a seed or bulb.

2. **Scoop up a pile of dirt** or mulch.

3. **Remove weeds** from a garden bed.

4. **Clear a small patch of snow** from a sidewalk.

5. **Move a pile** of leaves.

6. **Dig up a small plant** for transplanting.

7. **Level soil** in a garden bed.

8. **Create a small trench** for drainage.

9. **Dig out a small root** or rock.

10. **Mix compost** into garden soil.

11. **Edge a garden bed** by cutting through the grass.

12. **Fill in a small hole** or divot in the lawn.

13. **Collect debris** from a construction area.

14. **Move sand** from a sandbox.

15. **Rake leaves** into a pile (with the edge of the shovel).

16. **Remove old mulch** from a garden bed.

17. **Dig a small trench** for irrigation tubing.

18. **Move gravel** or small stones.

19. **Clear a spot** for a new plant.

20. **Mix fertilizer** into soil.

21. **Break up clumps of soil** in a garden.

22. **Create a small berm** for water management.

23. **Move garden soil** for a new bed or project.

24. **Cut through roots** that are obstructing an area.

25. **Transfer compost** to a garden bed.

26. **Shovel out the base** of a small plant for replanting.

27. **Level out a small area** for a garden path.

28. **Dig a small hole** for a post or stake.

29. **Clear a path** through a pile of debris.

30. **Fill a hole** with dirt or other materials.

Thirty Things in Thirty Seconds
You can do with a TRASH CAN

Trash cans are handy for quick clean-ups and organization around the house or yard!

1. **Dispose** of household waste.

2. **Collect recyclables** for sorting.

3. **Throw away food scraps** from meal prep.

4. **Organize trash for pickup** by separating items.

5. **Clear clutter** from a small area or desk.

6. **Dispose of garden debris** like leaves or branches.

7. **Toss out or recycle old newspapers** or magazines.

8. **Clean up after a party** by collecting used plates and cups.

9. **Remove packaging** from newly purchased items.

10. **Collect used tissues** or paper towels.

11. **Throw away** broken or damaged items.

12. **Collect pet waste** from a yard.

13. **Dispose of expired or unused medications** (in a designated way).

14. **Clear out** old food from the fridge.

15. **Dispose of packing peanuts** or bubble wrap.

16. **Collect worn-out or torn clothes** for donation.

17. **Clean up after a craft project** by disposing of scraps.

18. **Throw away used napkins** or disposable utensils.

19. **Collect trash from a car** before cleaning it.

20. **Organize a quick clean-up** by sorting items into bags.

21. **Throw away broken toys** or small household items.

22. **Dispose of small electronic waste** responsibly (if applicable).

23. **Remove expired food** from the pantry.

24. **Collect yard waste** like small twigs or grass clippings.

25. **Throw away** damaged or used wrapping paper.

26. **Dispose of** old or expired cosmetics.

27. **Clear out old receipts** or documents.

28. **Collect used cleaning cloths** or rags.

29. **Throw away empty containers** after using products.

30. **Dispose of** small amounts of construction debris.

Thirty Things in Thirty Seconds
You can do with a MOBILE PHONE

Mobile phones are incredibly versatile and can handle a wide range of tasks quickly!

1. **Send** a text message.

2. **Make a quick phone call.** Call someone back (but tell them you only have a few moments.)

3. **Check your email** for new messages.

4. **Take a photo** of something interesting.

5. **Open a navigation app** for directions.

6. **Check the weather** for your location.

7. **Set a timer** for a task or cooking.

8. **Look up a quick fact** on the internet.

9. **Send a quick message** via social media.

10. **Check your calendar** for upcoming events.

11. **Play a short song** or music clip.

12. **Record a voice memo** or note.

13. **Search for a nearby restaurant** or service.

14. **Check the latest news** headlines.

15. **Make a** quick online purchase.

16. **Update** your social media status.

17. **Set an alarm** for an important time.

18. **Find a recipe** for a meal.

19. **Check** your bank balance.

20. **Read a notification** from an app.

21. **Send a photo** via email or text.

22. **Review a recent call** or voicemail.

23. **Send a quick reply** in a group chat.

24. **Find and open a specific app** you need.

25. **Share a location** with a friend.

26. **Check your fitness tracker** stats.

27. **Look up** a contact's information.

28. **Scan a QR code**.

29. **Check** tomorrow's to-do list.

30. **Adjust phone settings** like brightness or volume.

Thirty Things in Thirty Seconds
You can do with a LABEL MAKER

Label makers are handy for organizing and identifying items quickly and efficiently!

1. **Create** a label for a file folder.

2. **Label a box** for storage.

3. **Tag a piece of equipment** with its name.

4. **Mark a shelf** with its contents.

5. **Identify** cables or wires.

6. **Label kitchen containers** (e.g., flour, sugar).

7. **Tag office supplies** like pens or folders.

8. **Create name tags** for an event or meeting.

9. **Label a storage bin** for toys or craft supplies.

10. **Mark a binder** with its subject.

11. **Tag a book** with its title or genre.

12. **Create a date label** for food storage.

13. **Label a plant pot** with its name or type.

14. **Tag a drawer** with its contents.

15. **Label a gift** with the recipient›s name.

16. **Mark a toolbox** with its contents.

17. **Create a label** for a home-made spice jar.

18. **Tag** a sports equipment bag.

19. **Identify a remote control** with its purpose.

20. **Label a pet's belongings** like a bed or toy.

21. **Create a nameplate** for a desk or office.

22. **Tag a donation box** with its contents.

23. **Label a calendar** for special events or reminders.

24. **Mark** a file cabinet drawer.

25. **Tag a set of keys** with their purpose.

26. **Label an electronics shelf** (e.g., batteries, chargers).

27. **Create a label** for a DIY project.

28. **Tag a drawer organizer** with its items.

29. **Label a personal journal** with your name.

30. **Mark a set of dishes** or kitchen utensils.

Thirty Things in Thirty Seconds
You can do with a FLASHLIGHT

A flashlight is a versatile tool for a variety of quick tasks in both every day and emergency situations!

1. **Illuminate** a dark room.

2. **Find something dropped** on the floor.

3. **Inspect a dark corner** or space.

4. **Read a map** or instruction manual in low light.

5. **Signal for help** or use as an emergency beacon.

6. **Check for leaks** or issues in dark areas.

7. **Find a keyhole** in the dark.

8. **Light up a camping area** briefly.

9. **Examine small details** on a project or craft.

10. **Spot wildlife** at night or in dark conditions.

11. **Locate a fuse box** or electrical panel.

12. **Look for something in your car** at night.

13. **Place one** near each entrance/exit of your house.

14. **Guide someone in the dark** or during a blackout.

15. **Check for pests** like insects or rodents.

16. **Inspect your attic** or basement.

17. **Light up a path** while walking at night.

18. **Find items in a backpack** or bag.

19. **Spot a power outage** or check an area without power.

20. **Illuminate a key area** for a quick repair or task.

21. **Check for mold or damage** in hidden areas.

22. **Light up a dark storage area** or closet.

23. **Use as a visual aid** for a presentation or explanation.

24. **Inspect car engine parts** or under the vehicle.

25. **Guide others in a group** during a nighttime event.

26. **Spot an address or house number** in the dark.

27. **Help with a nighttime** photo shoot.

28. **Check under furniture** or appliances.

29. **Light up a small outdoor area** for a quick task.

30. **Find your way around** during a power outage.

Thirty Things in Thirty Seconds
You can do while WAITING IN LINE

These quick activities can help pass the time, keep your mind engaged, or bring a moment of peace during a wait.

1. **Make a kind or humorous comment** to someone else in line.

2. **Take a look at your shopping list and your to-do list.** No need to wait until after you leave the store to remember what you forgot.

3. **Pick someone else** and just give them a knowing, pleasant smile.

4. **Take a moment for yourself** and stretch!

5. **Take another moment and breathe deep** . . . especially if you're getting anxious.

6. **Consciously stand straight and tall.** As you age, there is a tendency to tilt your head and neck downward. Aging: ward if off.

7. **Does your phone have a daily devotional?** Read it.

8. **Take a moment to be mindful** of all that is yours and be grateful.

9. **Remind yourself of what's coming**—check your calendar.

10. **Maybe you're hard pressed for time.** Glance at the time and plan what you'll do when you get through the line.

11. **Got groceries in your cart?** Plan your coming menu.

12. **What's not on your list that you want to do?** Set a goal and mentally prepare to achieve it.

13. **Still have your phone handy?** Take a moment and prep your home page.

14. **Look at your installed apps.** Delete any you don't use.

15. **Look around and enjoy** a list of pleasant memories.

16. **Make your brain work** by exercising it. Round up prices of items in your cart and estimate in approximate numbers how much your bill will be.

17. **Make a mental note of where you are** and think of stopping somewhere you had not planned on just to pick up a surprise for someone.

18. **Can you count your breaths** and change the rate for the better? You do this to calm and add peace to your soul.

19. **Still have that phone in your hand?** Clean it!

20. **Listen for background music** in the store. Does it calm you? Excite you? Make you want to leave or stay?

21. **Have a tough talk you need to with someone.** Plan it here while you have time to give it some significant thought.

22. **Not in a grocery store?** Think about items you need on a grocery list.

23. **Check your email** . . . anything important?

24. **Check for missed calls** that you need to return. Make a mental note; you don't want to call while in line.

25. **Need to send a short text** to someone? Do it!

26. **Send someone overlooked a note** saying you were thinking of them.

27. **Plan for an unexpected event.** Type in "Interesting things to do near me" into your phone's search bar.

28. **Trying to memorize something?** Practice it now.

29. **Got trash in your purse or bag?** Sort it and toss it.

30. **Take a moment and be grateful** that you have access to the things you are standing in line to buy.

About the Author

Gerald Robison has pastored churches on three continents, trained over 1,200 Bible teachers in over twenty-five countries, served as the international training manager for Walk Thru the Bible, and founded and cofounded three ministries.

He has instructed hundreds of mission classes, and has been a favorite speaker for Perspectives, Steeling the Mind conferences, and mission conferences around the nation and the world. He has worked with the Issachar Initiative, Finishing the Task, Perspectives, and City for the Nations.

Affectionately known as "Dr. G" to many, he has a deep foundation for ministry. He was called to ministry while still in high school and began preparations for it. He achieved his BA in psychology and counseling at Furman and Mercer Universities, his master's degree and his Doctor of Ministry at Luther Rice Seminary, another master's degree in education and counseling at Georgia State University, and more graduate studies at the International Institute of Theology and Law sponsored by Simon Greenleaf School of Law and the International Institute of Human Rights sponsored by the University of Strasbourg, France.

His passion is for helping reach people of every tongue, every tribe, and every nation until representatives from each group is gathered into the throne room of God for worshipping our heavenly Father.

Gerald (Dr. G) is a prolific author and has more on the way.